7-12

D1164606

The Emily Sonnets
The Life of Emily Dickinson

Text copyright © 2012 Jane Yolen
Illustrations copyright © 2012 Gary Kelley
Published in 2012 by Creative Editions
P.O. Box 227, Mankato, MN 56002 USA
Creative Editions is an imprint of The Creative Company
Edited by Aaron Frisch and Kate Riggs
Designed by Rita Marshall

Printed in Italy

Library of Congress Cataloging-in-Publication Data
Yolen, Jane.
The Emily sonnets: the life of Emily Dickinson / by Jane Yolen.
Summary: Acclaimed writer Jane Yolen employs 15 sonnets,
accompanied by brief biographical notes, to tell of the reclusive life
and literary innovations of 19th-century American poet Emily Dickinson.
ISBN 978-1-56846-215-8
1. Dickinson, Emily, 1830–1886–Poetry. I. Title.
PS3575.O43E55 2012
811'.54–dc23   2011040841

First edition
9 8 7 6 5 4 3 2 1

With thanks to the wonderful folks at the Emily Dickinson Museum in Amherst, especially Jane Wald,
executive director, who gave a careful reading to the manuscript of this book. "Emily Dickinson's House,"
with a few differences, was originally published in *The Horn Book*, May–June 2005.

The Emily Sonnets
The Life of Emily Dickinson

Jane Yolen

Illustrations by Gary Kelley

Creative Editions

Table of Contents

Author's Note

These poems, written over a period of seven years, spring from my love of the poet Emily Dickinson. I have always called her my neighbor, though we lived two towns and slightly more than fifty years apart.

I have visited her house—known as The Homestead—and her brother's house, The Evergreens, many times. Twice I had the opportunity to read her poems aloud in her garden, and another time I even recorded some of them in her broom closet. (The recordist insisted it had the best acoustics.)

In this book of sonnets about Emily's life, I have given each poem a title and an indication as to the speaker, whether Emily herself, her sister Lavinia (Vinnie), her niece Martha (Mattie), her mentor/friend Thomas Wentworth Higginson, an unknown critic, or me (JY). I have tried to tell the truth of her life, but as Emily said: "Tell all the Truth but tell it slant— / Success in Circuit lies …"

— Jane Yolen

The Brick House (Emily Speaks)

No house in town was built of brick

Except the one that bore me.

The roof was slant, the walls quite thick.

My mother did not adore me.

My father's smiles were rare and swift,

A grimace more than joy.

I was the second child, a gift;

The first one was a boy.

We two, like sailors in a storm,

Clung desperate to each other,

Trying to stay safe and warm,

Small sister to big brother;

He strove so hard my life to save

From drowning in that icy wave.

Sister Vinnie (Emily Speaks)

From the day that she was born

We have scarcely been apart.

Our love, though tried and sometimes worn,

Has long cocooned my art.

Our mother—cold as winter's core—

Still loved my sister most.

This burden Vinnie bravely bore

At quite a dreadful cost.

She had small time for ought but house

And for the family.

Like a scarecrow on a pole,

She saved the best for me.

She was for me both moon and sun.

We were two hearts that beat as one.

Educating Emily (Emily Speaks)

We sat our schooling row by row,

As if all knowledge comes in lines.

No one could tell me what to know,

And so I followed other signs.

I learned the spelling of the bee,

The mathematics of the rose.

I memorized the history

Of everything the garden grows.

And when my formal school was done,

I found more in the books of air;

My higher education won

From every bird found flying there.

My knowingness blooms day by day.

We each walk our particulate way.

14

Losing God, Finding God (Emily Speaks)

My family congregation was attendant unto God;

I alone did not accept that public notion.

I found Him in the garden and upon the greening sod.

I adored Him in the rivers and the ocean.

Heaven was above me, quite too far for my poor sight;

I preferred to keep my eyes upon the land.

Every Sunday as they went to church, I was prepared to fight

For the right to worship what was near at hand.

There were times I lost that battle and was hauled along as well,

Where half-heartedly I sang the morning hymn.

There my father, pure and terrible, did call upon his God,

Who was like him, both a Puritan and grim.

Yet if I must be an exile, shut from heaven evermore,

Still, I found God growing joyfully upon the earth's green floor.

Emily's Dog (Emily Speaks)

A shaggy ally, he often walked

Beside me to the other house.

And while I sat a spell and talked,

He lay as still as a mouse—

Though a thousand times the size.

When we marched back across the lawn

He could have chased the butterflies

Or raced a squirrel, and then been gone.

But never once he left my side,

Companioning with hulking grace.

Ignoring jays—their loud deride—

He turned up a devoted face

As true to me as sun that spills

Its farewell on the silent hills.

Chance Slips (Vinnie Speaks)

Emily reaches for several chance slips,

Bits of legal paper, gilt-edged sheets.

Then into the inkwell the pen she dips,

And measuring out her own heartbeats,

She scratches a line, gives it a dash—

Another follows, quick as the first.

Much like a wound, or a raw, bloody gash,

The poem on the page ends with a burst.

Poetry bleeds onto each tiny scrap,

Her perceptions all drawn line by line,

As if she has carefully painted a map

Of her heart, her mind, both gross and fine.

Then each is folded, stashed in a drawer.

Publication is too much like war.

The Myth (Emily Speaks)

What made me shut my door to life

Or love that might well grow,

Or any thought of being wife

Is long forgotten now.

I have my dog, my sister, kin,

My garden, and my stove.

I feel maintained within my skin,

'Tis all I care of love.

And letters from friends near and far

To tantalize my mind,

As well as books and poetry

Made fine by womankind.

What need for me an open door

When in myself is so much more?

White Dress (The Critic Speaks)

There is no surprise in her white dress,

As there is no surprise in habit.

Some would say she used it to suppress

Her gender, to cushion her rabid

Tongue, to turn away a would-be wooer,

Or to confuse the envious neighbors

Who wished to visit and to view her,

Thinking she owed them notice or favors.

But sometimes a white dress is only that,

It keeps the daily choices few.

No need for laces, gloves, or hat.

Now any long white dress will do.

As uniform, it simplifies

A life that slants itself with lies.

Hedges (Emily Speaks)

My soldiers, steady in a row,

Their helmets verdigrised by God,

Wearing epaulettes of crow,

Their feet eclipsed within the sod.

Who dares to go whereon they stand?

No strangers can trespass their line,

For they patrol as I command,

And all they guard is surely mine.

My house they safe from prying eyes.

My brother's house they likewise keep.

And in their stiff and green disguise

They stay awake while others sleep.

When fear's the driver, all are driven.

This war there is no quarter given.

The Poet Asks (Thomas Wentworth Higginson Answers)

Yes, Dear Friend, your verses live,

They parse the years, they stretch the miles.

They sing at weddings where they give

The bride an arm along the aisles.

They solemn stand at funerals

And dirge the dead men down to sod.

They count, like holy numerals,

The way we calibrate our God.

Yes, Dear Friend, your verses stay.

The fascicles you left behind,

Hand-stitched and hidden, in a way

Are marvels of poetic kind.

In verses yet you still abide,

Though gone from here, you have not died.

Yes, Sue, Yes (Emily Speaks)

Yes, Sue, yes—you were the muse

Who edited the poet's art.

And yes, Sue, yes—you got to choose

The Dickinson who held your heart.

You kept with care the fragile peace

That stretched across the trampled lawn.

You counted out the sure increase

Of poems I wrote into the dawn.

If History has near effaced

Your presence in this poet's life,

And casual readers have erased

Your role except as brother's wife,

Dear Emily has this to say:

You *were* my sister, just a hedge away.

Ardor for the Lie (The Critic Speaks)

Was it just lies she loved to tell,

Or some strange landscape longed to find?

Each poem rings through me like a bell,

Each line blows hot and cold like wind,

Like breath from an enchanted lung.

To read her is to sail the miles

To skies where heaven's spheres have sung,

Her feet well planted in far isles.

And in the frigate of her poems

We circumnavigate the Earth,

Yet never leave our simple homes.

Just think how much such lies are worth.

What honor is to poets due

When liars tell the deeper true.

Our Fairy Aunt (Mattie Speaks)

When we were young, we thought her fey,

The blood of faerie threading her veins,

Though human in all other ways.

Like Queen Mab who endless reigns,

Upon the hillside, there she flitted,

White-clad shadow, potent queen.

Into our circumscribed lives she fitted

Not grown, not child, but in-between.

We iced her cakes, the dark warm plums,

Snatched caramels from her patient hands.

And in the cool cellar stole such crumbs

From lawless cakes, our prodigal demands.

And she, both queen and moonlit knight,

Would take our parts though wrong the fight.

1,775 Poems (Vinnie Speaks)

So much of her laid out in poems,

In short lines and in long.

So much of her in slanted rhymes.

Instead of a life—these songs.

Some forty manuscripts I found

That I could not destroy,

For writing them had been her bond,

Her hope, her heart, her joy.

I cannot make my sister live,

But neither let her go.

I cannot to the fire give

Her poems, for this I know:

What I found here upon these pages,

Must be published for the ages.

Emily Dickinson's House (JY Speaks)

Two towns away, there is a street

Where poems and their readers meet;

A place a lady poet stood

Amidst the clapboard, brick, and wood.

And sometimes most emphatically,

The risk of immortality

Was written while she skimmed the milk,

Or mended clothes with threads of silk.

She looked around, eight windows wide,

While rarely venturing outside,

But inside—where her poems took place—

She gave the world a fine embrace.

So if you visit, take a breath.

Inhale the poems beyond her death.

Emily After

Only a few people—mostly family and friends—ever read a poem by Emily Dickinson before she died in 1886, but today she is one of the most famous of American poets. So many poets have written poems to Emily and about her that she has become as much muse as poet. Novelists, playwrights, and moviemakers have also composed works about her, and literary scholars and researchers have mined every inch of her existence for facts. Emily's relatively short life was defined largely by short poems. And so I end not with a sonnet but with a short poem about her. (JY)

Emily Dickinson stayed at home—

And each day wrote a little poem.

A little poem each day turns out

To be a lot to write about.

Notes

The Brick House (Emily Speaks)
Emily Elizabeth Dickinson was born in Amherst, Massachusetts, on December 10, 1830, in one of the first brick houses in town. Her brother Austin had been born a year and a half earlier. At that time, one of the female children in a family was often considered a "gift" and was supposed to remain unwed to care for her parents as they aged. Emily's mother, Emily Norcross Dickinson, was distant, suffering from depression. Emily wrote: "I always ran Home to Awe [Austin] when a child, if anything befell me. He was an awful Mother, but I liked him better than none." Some scholars think she actually might have been referring to her father, Edward Dickinson, with this remark, since he was the parent who gave her some comfort and attention. Edward was a prominent Amherst lawyer who so rarely smiled that when he did—as Emily wrote to a friend—his smiles were almost "embarrassing."

Sister Vinnie (Emily Speaks)
Lavinia ("Vinnie") Norcross Dickinson, Emily's younger sister, was the family enabler. As the eldest girl, the housekeeping should have been primarily Emily's job. Instead, Vinnie was the one who took on the role of domestic caretaker as soon as she was old enough. This allowed Emily the time to write, so she depended on Vinnie as much as any other member of the family did. Vinnie wrote later that Emily "had to think—she was the only one of us who had that to do." Neither girl ever married, and their brother, when he wed, built a house right next door. After her sister died, Vinnie reminisced, "Ever since we were little girls we have been wonderfully dear to each other—and many times when desirable offers of marriage have been made to Emily she has said—I have never seen anyone that I cared for as much as you Vinnie."

Educating Emily (Emily Speaks)
The Dickinsons were strong advocates for children's education—for both boys and girls. Emily's early schooling consisted of work in classic literature, Latin, mathematics, history, and botany. After attending Amherst Academy, where she excelled, she left home in 1847 for Mount Holyoke Female Seminary in South Hadley, ten miles away. There, beset by homesickness, she had a difficult time, and when—along with forty other girls—she wouldn't sign an oath publicly professing faith in Christ, she was given a tongue-lashing by the head of the school. After the year was out, Emily did not return to Mount Holyoke, choosing—like many girls of her time—to end her formal education at that point. However, she continued to read widely and learn much for the rest of her life.

Losing God, Finding God (Emily Speaks)
The Dickinsons attended Amherst's First Congregational Church, but Emily did not hold with the worshipful ways of New England Puritans. She once wrote of her father that "his heart was pure and terrible"—a description often used for Puritans—though she certainly found him more attentive than her mother, even to the point of being controlling. At both home and at school, she felt pressured to join the ranks of the "saved." Although she never became a regular churchgoer, it worried her enough that she once wrote about "being shut out of heaven." She started another poem, "Some keep the Sabbath going to Church— / I keep it, staying at Home." Another states: "At least—to pray—is left—is left— / Oh Jesus—in the Air— / I know not which Thy Chamber is— / I'm knocking everywhere ..."

Emily's Dog (Emily Speaks)
Emily's faithful dog was a giant Newfoundland her father gave her in 1849. They often walked together between The Homestead and her brother's house next door—The Evergreens. Her father thought the dog, which needed daily runs, might help Emily overcome her fear of going out in public. She named the animal Carlo, after a dog in her favorite novel, *Jane Eyre*, writing about him to Thomas

Wentworth Higginson: "You ask of my companions. Hills, sir, and the sundown, and a dog large as myself, that my father bought me. They are better than beings because they know, but do not tell...." Carlo kept her company for seventeen years—a long life for such a large dog. After he died in January 1866, she grieved mightily and could never bring herself to get another dog.

Chance Slips (Vinnie Speaks)

Emily's first poems were fairly ordinary. "Awake ye muses nine, sing me a strain divine" is from her earliest known poem, dated March 4, 1850, when she was twenty. It was published two years later in the *Springfield Republican*. As the years went on, Emily experimented with slant rhyme—ending lines with words that almost rhyme, like soul/all or theme/time. Her punctuation became her own, and she often used dashes instead of periods or commas and capitalized nouns, proper or not. Around 1858, she began to write on what her niece Martha called "any chance slip of paper, ... sometimes a gilt-edged sheet with a Paris mark, often a random scrap of commercial note from her Father's law office." These she assembled into dozens of packets—bound with needle and thread—which editor Mabel Loomis Todd would later call "fascicles." Emily wrote almost eighteen hundred poems altogether but published fewer than fifteen in her lifetime. She declared in one poem that "Publication—is the Auction / Of the Mind of Man."

The Myth (Emily Speaks)

Emily wrote "The Soul selects her own Society—Then—shuts the Door ..." around the time she turned her back on the greater Amherst community. This reclusive life began when she was about thirty. Eventually, she stopped seeing anyone besides her family and their servants, speaking to visitors from behind a door. Her neighbors called her "The Myth." Still, she was not entirely a hermit. She visited at The Evergreens next door until the 1860s at least and later played with her niece and nephews in her own house. She even lowered homemade cakes and sweets in a basket down to the neighborhood children. Her niece wrote about her "droll humor" and about her being "a nimble as well as loving ally." Emily read constantly and carried on ardent correspondences with many friends. But what she was most passionate about was "the Art, within the Soul."

White Dress (The Critic Speaks)

Emily's white dress is almost as famous as her poems. She began wearing white sometime after 1862. Emily was extremely uneasy about being touched by a stranger, so—reportedly—someone else her size had to be measured for the fittings. Although she had several similar white dresses, only one has survived. An exact replica of that dress was made for the museum that now occupies The Homestead. Perhaps Emily dressed in white as a walking metaphor, an angel of poetry. As she wrote: "For such, the Angels go— / Rank after Rank, with even feet—And Uniforms of Snow." Scholars, poets, and critics have described her white dress alternately as symbolizing a wedding gown, a shroud, a hospital gown, a nun's habit, or a ghost's sheet.

Hedges (Emily Speaks)

In historical photographs, the hemlock hedge that runs across the front of the Dickinson property stands smartly at attention. Hemlocks are evergreens, and another word for their kind of deep green color is "verdigris." With a wooden fence fronting it like a shield, that hedge—planted in the 1860s and originally nine hundred feet long—acted as a stern guardian of the house. The Emily Dickinson Museum Web site states that "the original design intent for the hedge was to allow a clear view of the upper stories of both homes, while shielding the gardens from casual view by passersby." After the death of the last of the Dickinsons, individual trees in the fence grew huge. In 2009, an extensive restoration project replanted the hedge and replaced the fence.

The Poet Asks
(Thomas Wentworth Higginson Answers)

In 1862, Emily sent four of her poems to author Thomas Wentworth Higginson, asking, "Are you too deeply occupied to say if my Verse is alive?" This was in response to a recently published article of his in the literary magazine *The Atlantic Monthly*. The poems sent included "Safe in their alabaster chambers" and "I'll tell you how the sun rose." Higginson made some suggestions for revision which Emily called "surgery," but it was the first time she had had an honest evaluation from someone outside the immediate family, and she valued his input. From that moment, he became her mentor, though he warned Emily against publication because her poetry was so unconventional. It was ironic, then, that he helped edit the first two volumes of her poems published after her death.

Yes, Sue, Yes (Emily Speaks)
Susan Gilbert Dickinson ("Sue"), Austin's wife, was as close to Emily as any blood sister. Even though her marriage to Austin became seriously frayed over the years, Sue's friendship with Emily endured, despite having its own fractures. The two women sent notes back and forth across the lawn, and in one, Emily wrote, "The tie between us is very fine, but a hair never dissolves." Also, in a poem, Emily said, "One Sister have I in our house, / And one, a hedge away." A published writer of stories, Sue was shown many of Emily's poems when other family members were not because Emily trusted her response. They were so close that the last thing Emily ever wrote to her was, "My answer is an unmitigated Yes Sue!" though we do not know to what this refers.

Ardor for the Lie (The Critic Speaks)
Emily wrote about her eldest nephew Edward ("Ned") that "Ned tells that the Clock purrs and the Kitten ticks. He inherits his Uncle Emily's ardor for the lie." (She often called herself "Uncle Emily" as a family joke.) By that, she meant that love of wordplay, metaphor, and even the making of a poem were conscious lies that led in the end to Truth. Ned was a good writer, inheriting some of her talent. Unfortunately, he suffered from epilepsy, which may have weakened his heart, and he died from angina at thirty-seven. Still, he outlived his beloved aunt by twelve years, long enough to see her poetry published. One of the poems in her book begins: "There is no Frigate like a Book …" suggesting that one can more easily, cheaply, and deeply travel the world by reading books than by setting off on a frigate, or ship.

Our Fairy Aunt (Mattie Speaks)
Although often portrayed as a brooding recluse, Emily had an enchanting side she shared with Austin and Sue's children: Ned, Martha ("Mattie"), and Gilbert (known as "Gib"). She played with them and encouraged their occasional naughtiness. Mattie later wrote that Emily once

"purloined" a box of maple sugar from the family supply and sent it to the children with these instructions: "Omit to return box. Omit to know you received box." Mattie explained that, to them, "she was of fairy lineage, akin to the frost on the nursery pane in Winter or the humming bird or Midsummer." Emily's favorite, Gib, died tragically at age eight of typhoid. The heartbroken aunt wrote to his mother, Sue, "I see him in the Stars and meet his sweet velocity in everything that flies." She never recovered from his death. Mattie was the only child of Sue and Austin's to live into old age—well into the twentieth century—and helped publish volumes of her aunt's poetry.

1,775 Poems (Vinnie Speaks)
Vinnie discovered more than forty hand-sewn manuscripts after Emily's death, and the number of known poems stood at 1,775 for many years. According to the latest scholarly count, that number is now 1,789 and includes verses found in her letters to family, friends, mentors, and other people she greatly admired. Despite promising to destroy Emily's personal papers, Vinnie could not bring herself to burn the poems. Instead, she asked two of Emily's friends—Thomas Wentworth Higginson and Mabel Loomis Todd—to edit the poetry. They smoothed out Emily's odd punctuation and even odder capitalizations. In 1890, the first book, *Poems*, was published by Roberts Brothers, Boston. Within two years, it had gone through eleven editions. Later scholars restored Emily's now iconic dashes and capitalized nouns. Emily once wrote a poem that began, "This is my letter to the world / That never wrote to me." Since that time, hundreds of books have been written *about* her, and her poetry is beloved around the world.

Emily Dickinson's House (JY Speaks)
There is an eight-windowed cupola atop The Homestead where Emily sat, read Shakespeare, and possibly wrote, her dog Carlo at her feet. Although she did little venturing outside the Dickinson properties once her reclusiveness took hold, her poems spanned the universe, such as the one that begins: "I lost a World—the other day! / Has anybody found? / You'll know it by the Row of Stars / Around its forehead bound."